I Am the Land, These Are My People

An All-Ages Naturalist Coloring StoryBook
of the Inland Northwest

Written and Compiled by Rosalee and Xavier de la Forêt
Illustrations by Caitlin Cordell

Published by Methow Press
P.O. Box 1213, Twisp, WA 98856
www.methowpress.com

Printed in the United States of America

ISBN: 979-8-9913567-6-3

Artwork by Caitlin Cordell. Used by permission.

Methow Press
Twisp, Washington 98856

Introduction

This coloring storybook aims to bridge the past, present, and future of what is commonly called the Inland Northwest, and to inspire people to get to know and appreciate all the life forms who contribute to its life cycles through the seasons.

First and foremost, we acknowledge and express our gratitude for the ancestors who transformed and shaped this landscape from bare rock uncovered by melting glaciers to one populated with a great diversity and abundance of beings. Indigenous people have followed the lichens, plants, trees, birds, and animals who gradually moved here, and have been taking care of this place for thousands of years.

When we stand on a hillside full of wild foods and medicine, we like to think that, many hundred years ago, a person stood in the same place thinking about how to tend to it so that the future generations—us, now—would have a beautiful and abundant place to call home. For that we are extremely grateful.

We are grateful and honored to live on traditional mətxʷu (Methow) land. In an effort to honor the indigenous people of this land, we thank Elaine Timentwa Emerson, an esteemed tribal elder, for providing the traditional nsəlxcin names of the beings in this book that she knows, with her preferred spelling. We encourage you to connect with the indigenous people and language of where you live to deepen your appreciation of all the forces that have shaped your landscape.

We also thank *you* for picking up this book and sharing it with the people in your life. We hope it will encourage you to appreciate and learn more about all the beings who contribute to the health, beauty, and abundance of this land, and that it will inspire you and the next generations to take an active part in being good caretakers.

We sincerely hope that many hundred years from now, a person will stand on this same hillside, look at the marvelous landscape, and express gratitude to all of *us* for making the choices that contributed to their wellbeing.

I am the land,
and these are my people through the seasons...

Deep snow covers the mountains, creating a winter playland for wolverines and lynx who are well adapted to live in these harsh conditions.

Do you see the pine martens? They like to climb trees to hunt. Many birds head south for the winter, but Steller's jays and Clark's nutcrackers are at home in the snowy mountains.

What birds do you notice in the winter?
Can you name the mountain peaks near you?

Common English Names	Latin Binomial	nsəlxcin
Subalpine fir	*Abies lasiocarpa*	məŕiłp
Engelmann spruce	*Picea engelmannii*	ċəq́ċəq́iłməlx
Western conifer seed bug	*Leptoglossus occidentalis*	
Clark's nutcracker	*Nucifraga columbiana*	
Steller's jay	*Cyanocitta stelleri*	qʷʕásqiʔ
Wolverine	*Gulo luscus*	q̇ʷəłtmin
Lynx	*Lynx canadensis*	wápupxən
Marten	*Martes americana*	ṗəṗiq̇s

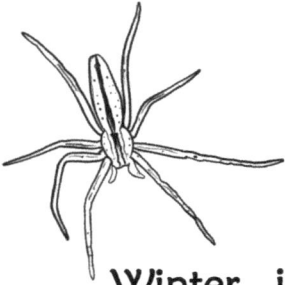

Some of my people sleep through the cold dark winter months, while others flourish in the thick snows.

Winter is a time for rest and play. Humans glide on their skis while great horned owls silently watch from above. The snowshoe hares have turned from brown to white so they can blend in with the snow. Flickers peck through bark in search of food. "Rap! Rap! Rap!" Nuthatches, like weightless magicians, walk up and down trees.

Who is awake near you? Who is hibernating?

Common English Names	Latin Binomial	nsəlxcin
Ponderosa pine	*Pinus ponderosa*	sʕatkʷəłp
Douglas fir	*Pseudotsuga menziesii*	cq̓iłp
Slender crab spider	*Tibellus oblongus*	túpəlaʔ
Great horned owl	*Bubo virginianus*	snínaʔ
Northern flicker	*Colaptes auratus*	kʷəlkʷaʕqn
White-breasted nuthatch	*Sitta carolinensis*	
Snowshoe hare	*Lepus americanus*	spəplínaʔ
Mule deer	*Odocoileus hemionus*	tíwłca
Ermine	*Mustela erminea*	spȧpłqcaʔ
Yellow-pine chipmunk	*Tamias amoenus*	q̓ʷəq̓ʷc̓wiyaʔ
Human	*Homo sapiens*	sqilxʷ

The rivers are edged with ice, yet still filled with life.

Look! The otter caught a fish. A kingfisher is on the hunt while merganser ducks float downstream.

As the sun's rays grow longer every day, plant life begins to emerge. Cottonwood, willow, and alder buds swell; their leaves and flowers await the early signs of spring before they emerge.

Can you see signs of a beaver?
Will the otter share his fish with the bald eagle?

Common English Names	Latin Binomial	nsəlxcin
Black cottonwood	*Populus trichocarpa*	mulx
Scouler's willow	*Salix scouleriana*	paʕpaʕíłp
Mountain alder	*Alnus incant ssp. Tenuifolia*	kiʔkiʔtníłp
Belted kingfisher	*Ceryle alcyon*	ċəris
Common merganser	*Mergus merganser*	xʷʕatxʷət
Bald eagle	*Haliaeetus leucocephalus*	pəqlqin
River otter	*Lutra canadensis*	lətkʷ

The soils begin to thaw with the spring equinox. Snow caps the distant mountains but is melting fast on the valley floor. Mud season is here!

"Poke-your-neighbor!" Can you hear the red-winged blackbirds sing out in their marshy territories?

They're not the only ones celebrating warmer temperatures. Mallard ducks arrive from their southern dwellings while muskrats peek out from the cattails and shore willows.

Common English Names	Latin Binomial	nsəlxcin
Cattail	*Typha latifolia*	q̓ʷəsq̓ʷəsqin
Pacific willow	*Salix lasiandra*	stəkcxʷiłp
Aspen	*Populus tremuloides*	məlməltiłp
Mourning cloak	*Nymphalis antiopa*	pəlpalẃicyaʔ
Red-winged blackbird	*Agelaius phoeniceus*	xʷəlxʷəláʕkn
Mallard	*Anas platyrhynchos*	nkʷytilps
Muskrat	*Ondatra zibethica*	saʕnixʷ

As the snow melts, early spring flowers emerge. Songbirds return from their winter voyages while marmots sun themselves on rocky slopes. The western tiger swallowtail drinks nectar from the flowers.

Have you found the first buttercup flower blooming? When do the phoebes and robins arrive near you?

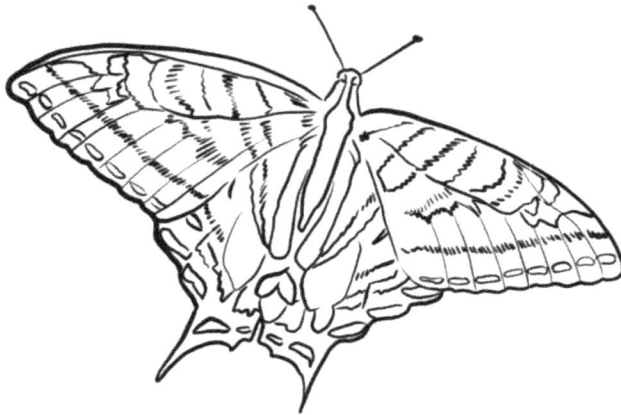

Common English Names	Latin Binomial	nsəlxcin
Crocus	Crocus spp.	
Buttercup	Ranunculus glaberrimus	skəńiŕmən
Great mullein	Verbascum thapsus	
Western tiger swallowtail	Papilio rutulus	pəlpalẃícyaʔ
Say's phoebe	Sayornis saya	
American robin	Turdus migratorius	ʕʷəsʕʷisxaʔ
Violet-green swallow	Tachycineta thalassina	mamqʷcən
Northern pocket gopher	Thomomys talpoides	púłłaʔxʷ
Yellow-bellied marmot	Marmota flaviventris	sk̓ʷuyk̓ʷuy

Colors erupt with blooming flowers everywhere. The rubber boa slithers gently through the vibrant leaves and flowers of the chocolate tips while a vole freezes nearby, hoping to escape detection. Meadowlarks sing sweetly in the meadow while bright bluebirds captivate the eye.

What are your favorite spring flowers? The delicate spring beauties? The nodding bluebells and yellow bells? The puff of a waterleaf?

Which of these are food? Which are medicine?

Common English Names	Latin Binomial	nsəlxcin
Bluebells	*Mertensia longiflora*	
Spring beauties	*Claytonia lanceolata*	skʷənkʷinəm
Yellow bells	*Fritillaria pudica*	ʕaʔtmən
Chocolate tips	*Lomatium dissectum*	ʔáyuʔ
Shooting stars	*Dodecatheon conjugens*	sk̓ʷək̓ʷúyk̓ʷuy
Waterleaf	*Hydrophyllum capitatum*	
Rubber boa	*Charina bottae*	
Western bluebird	*Sialia Mexicana*	qʷʕaymíls
Western meadowlark	*Sturnella neglecta*	waʕwíckʷlaʔ
Meadow vole	*Microtus pennsylvanicus*	

Do you hear that? The chorus frogs sing lullabies each night with their mating calls. The sagebrush steppe is filled with a deep bass-like beat, "Gu-gu-gug." The dusky grouse puts on a vivid display amongst blooming saskatoon and Oregon grape shrubs.

Mary captures the brilliant displays of spring in her heart and photos.

Common English Names	Latin Binomial	nsəlxcin
Larkspur	*Delphinium nuttallianum*	
Saskatoon	*Amelanchier alnifolia*	siyaʔ
Tall oregon-grape	*Mahonia aquifolium*	sćəŕsiɫməɫ
Sweat bee	*Agapostemon texanus*	
Pacific tree frog	*Pseudacris regilla*	sẇaŕákxən
Rufous-sided towhee	*Pipilo erythrophthalmus*	
Dark-eyed junco	*Junco hyemalis*	
Blue grouse	*Dendragapus obscurus*	xʷaʔxʷaʔyúɫ
Human	*Homo sapiens*	sqilxʷ

The hillsides are covered in the brilliant colors of yellow arrowleaf balsamroot and purple lupines, but there is danger amongst the beauty. A rattlesnake warns that he feels threatened, while a black widow crawls further back into her nest.

Do you hear the piercing call of the red tail hawk's cry?

A long-tailed weasel ducks into the thick flowers. Safe for another day.

Common English Names	Latin Binomial	nsəlxcin
Arrowleaf balsamroot	*Balsamorhiza sagittata*	smúkʷaʔxən
Lupine	*Lupinus sericeus*	wəswásxənqən
Narrow-leaved desert-parsley	*Lomatium triternatum*	
Bitterbrush	*Purshia tridentata*	
Bitterroot	*Lewisia rediviva*	spiƛ̓əm
Painted lady	*Vanessa cardui*	pəl̓pal̓w̓ícyaʔ
Western black widow	*Latrodectus hesperus*	
Pacific rattlesnake	*Crotalus oreganus*	xaʔx̌ʔúlaʔxʷ
Swainson's hawk	*Buteo swainsoni*	l̓əl̓íkl̓ək
Townsend warbler	*Dendroica townsendi*	
Long-tailed weasel	*Mustela frenata*	ƚk̓am

Shhhh! Be very quiet, the fawn is sleeping. Her mom is probably somewhere nearby—best to stay here and watch from a distance. The painted turtle suns himself by the lakeshore, amidst the spring blooms.

Who do you see? Arnica? Mariposa lily? Fairy slippers? Violets?

Do you see the crossbill flying above the lake? What a funny beak! What kind of food do you think they like to eat? What are you eating this time of year? Have you found any morel mushrooms?

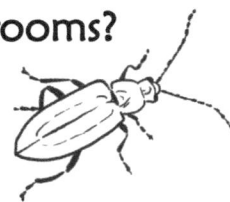

Common English Names	Latin Binomial	nsəlxcin
Morels	Morchella snyderi	
Indian paintbrush	Castilleja miniata	
Fairy slippers	Calypso bulbosa	
Heart-leaved arnica	Arnica cordifolia	
Stream violet	Viola Glabella	
Western mugwort	Artemisia ludoviciana	
Mariposa lily	Calochortus lyallii	
Buckwheat	Eriogonum douglasii	
Green beetle	Scelolyperus schwarzii	
Painted turtle	Chrysemys picta	ʔaṙsíkʷ
Red crossbill	Loxia curvirostra	
Pileated woodpecker	Dryocopus pileatus	pʷaɬqən
Swainson's thrush	Catharus ustulatus	
Whitetail deer	Odocoileus virginianus	ɬukʷtúps

It's time to plant garden veggies!

Everyone is busy in the garden, from the buzzing hummingbirds to the sunbathing garter snake. The mole aerates the soil while the house wren sings a beautiful song.

It's time to make lilac bouquets!

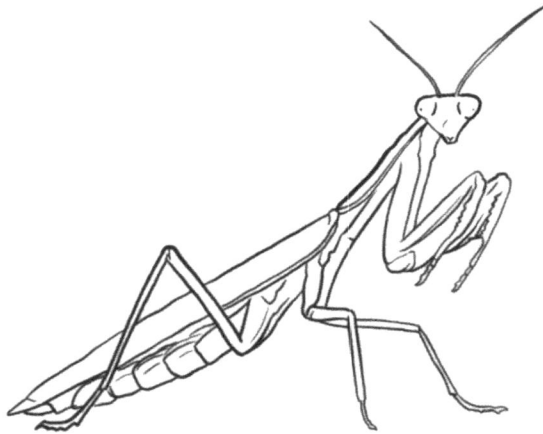

Common English Names	Latin Binomial	nsəlxcin
Lilac	*Syringa vulgaris*	
Large-flowered collomia	*Collomia grandiflora*	
Diffuse knapweed	*Centaurea diffusa*	
Mock orange	*Philadelphus lewisii*	wəxwáxiłp
Praying mantis	*Mantis religiosa*	
Common garter snake	*Thamnophis sirtalis*	skʷəkʷawílxaʔ
Rufous hummingbird	*Selasphorus rufus*	x̌ʷənamx̌ʷnam
House wren	*Troglodytes aedon*	naxxaɫ
Western tanager	*Piranga ludoviciana*	
Pacific mole	*Scapanus orarius*	púɫyaʔ

Do you see footprints on the ground?
Who will we see further along the trail?

The tracks on the left look like tiny bear prints, but they're actually left by a skunk! The other tracks are from a moose who might be eating in the meadow ahead.

There are so many pretty flowers to visit. Tiger lilies, lady's slippers, and yarrow fill forests and meadows. Take time to smell the wild roses. But watch out for pesky mosquitoes!

Common English Names	Latin Binomial	nsəlxcin
Trembling aspen	*Populus tremuloides*	məlməltiłp
Lady's slippers	*Cypripedium montanum*	
Nootka rose	*Rosa nutkana*	skʷəkʷiłp
Blue elderberry	*Sambucus caerulea*	ćqʷikʷ
Yarrow	*Achillea millefolium*	
Snowbrush	*Ceanothus velutinus*	
Tiger lily	*Lilium columbianum*	
Death camas	*Zigadenus venenosus*	yíwistən
Cool weather mosquito	*Culiseta incidens*	slaqs
Gopher snake	*Pituophis catenifer*	sx̣ʷiyúps
Red-headed woodpecker	*Melanerpes erythrocephalus*	caqyalqn
Lazuli bunting	*Passerina amoena*	
Northern goshawk	*Accipiter gentilis*	
Striped skunk	*Mephitis mephitis*	snəkstíyaʔ
Moose	*Alces alces*	paʕpaʕláċaʔ

The summer sun is hot on the valley floor, but the air is cooler in the mountains. Go quietly! Otherwise the pika will chirp and alarm everyone to your presence. The growing season is short up high. The hoary marmots are fighting for mates just as the flowers are bursting from their winter slumber.

Which flower looks like an elephant's head?
What do you think the golden eagle sees from her high perch?

Common English Names	Latin Binomial	nsəlxcin
Western larch	*Larix occidentalis*	ciqʷlx
Sitka valerian	*Valeriana sitchensis*	məsáwiʔ
Monkey flower	*Mimulus guttatus*	
Monkshood	*Aconitum columbianum*	
Cow parsnip	*Heracleum lanatum*	xʷəxʷtiɬp
False hellebore	*Veratrum viride*	sliq̇mən
Elephant's head	*Pedicularis groenlandica*	
Horse fly	*Tabanus stonei*	skəkaʕtəlqs
Grey jay	*Perisoreus canadensis*	qʷʕásqiʔ
Golden eagle	*Aquila chrysaetos*	məlqnups
Mountain goat	*Oreamnos americanus*	sx̌ʷəƛ̓iʔ
Pika	*Ochotona princeps*	
Hoary marmot	*Marmota caligata*	xʷíwxʷəw
Aplodontia	*Aplodontia rufia*	

Do you smell smoke from a distant fire? It's hot and dry in the summer but kayaks, salmon, and lamprey share the cool river. On the riverside quail cry out, "Cheee-cah-go."

It's time to fill your baskets with saskatoon berries,
while giving thanks for the bounty of summer.

Common English Names	Latin Binomial	nsəlxcin
Saskatoon	*Amelanchier alnifolia*	siyaʔ
Big sagebrush	*Artemisia tridentata*	qʷəlqʷəlqin
Alfalfa	*Medicago sativa*	yiŕyiŕqín
Showy milkweed	*Asclepias speciosa*	sənk̓lip lʔ‿sṕićəns
Goldenrod crab spider	*Misumena vatia*	
Turkey vulture	*Cathartes aura*	
Red-tailed hawk	*Buteo jamaicensis*	piyaʔ
American dipper	*Cinclus mexicanus*	
California quail	*Callipepla californica*	ćəćlaʕʷsqən
Spring chinook	*Oncorhynchus tshawytscha*	ntytyix
Pacific lamprey	*Entosphenus tridentatus*	kʷutwən
Human	*Homo sapiens*	sqilxʷ

Even at night many beings are busy by the moonlight to escape the heat of the day. Bears, coyotes, and humans all want a share of the tasty chokecherries and hawthorn berries while bats and nighthawks hunt the skies.

What star constellations do you see in the sky?

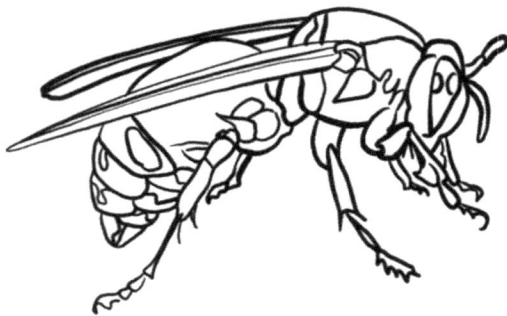

Common English Names	Latin Binomial	nsəlxcin
Chokecherry	*Prunus virginiana*	łəxʷłaǎ
Goldenrod	*Solidago canadensis*	
Yellow dock	*Rumex crispus*	
Bald-faced hornet	*Dolichovespula maculata*	
Black hawthorn	*Crataegus douglasii*	swaʔník
Common nighthawk	*Chordeiles minor*	pʕas
Mourning dove	*Zenaida macroura*	həḿíshəḿis
Coyote	*Canis latrans*	sənk̓lip
Black bear	*Ursus americanus*	skəḿxist
Little brown myotis	*Myotis lucifugus*	
Human	*Homo sapiens*	sqilxʷ

Splash! Was that a rainbow trout or an otter?

At the height of summer it's refreshing to take a plunge in an alpine lake! Fireweed, cattails, and tule line the shore and the lake is teeming with life. Fish swim below, dragonflies zip over the surface, and flycatcher birds feast.

Keep an eye on your picnic food!
Otherwise the ground squirrels may steal it.

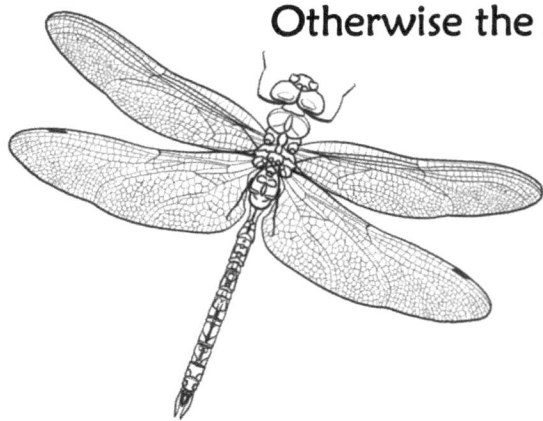

Common English Names	Latin Binomial	nsəlxcin
Fireweed	*Epilobium angustifolium*	
Tule	*Scirpus lacustris*	tukʷtaṅ
Water hemlock	*Cicuta douglasii*	yinixʷ
Cattail	*Typha latifolia*	q̇ʷəsq́ʷəsqin
Blue-eyed darner	*Rhionaeschna multicolor*	
Rainbow trout	*Oncorhynchus mykiss*	xʷumína?
Pacific-slope flycatcher	*Empidonax difficilis*	
Warbling vireo	*Vireo gilvus*	
River otter	*Lutra canadensis*	lətkʷ
Golden-mantled squirrel	*Citellus lateralis*	?a?ísck̇

The geese are already headed south.
Can you hear their honking songs fill the sky?

Meanwhile, waxwings feast on bountiful rose hips,
spreading their seeds far and wide.

A cougar quietly scans the horizon.
What will she have for lunch?

Common English Names	Latin Binomial	nsəlxcin
Nootka rose	Rosa nutkana	skʷəkʷiɬp
European paper wasp	Polistes dominula	sqʷuʔɬ
Cedar waxwing	Bombycilla cedrorum	
Canada goose	Branta canadensis	k̓ʷəsixʷ
Cougar	Felis concolor	swaʕ

As the days grow shorter and the air becomes cool and crisp, let's give thanks for the bountiful harvest. Apples are picked from the orchard. Squash and onions are cured in the fields for winter storage as the last of the beans and corn are picked. Squirrels and mice scamper to glean the leftover bounty while flocks of turkeys roam the fields.

What are your favorite harvest foods?

Common English Names	Latin Binomial	nsəlxcin
Two-striped grasshopper	*Melanoplus bivittatus*	ćańćəṅ
Wild turkey	*Meleagris gallopavo*	łət̓ʷłutqs
Chipping sparrow	*Spizella passerina*	
Bushy-tailed woodrat	*Neotoma cinerea*	hiẇt
Red squirrel	*Tamiasciurus hudsonicus*	ʔaʔíscḱ
Human	*Homo sapiens*	sqilxʷ

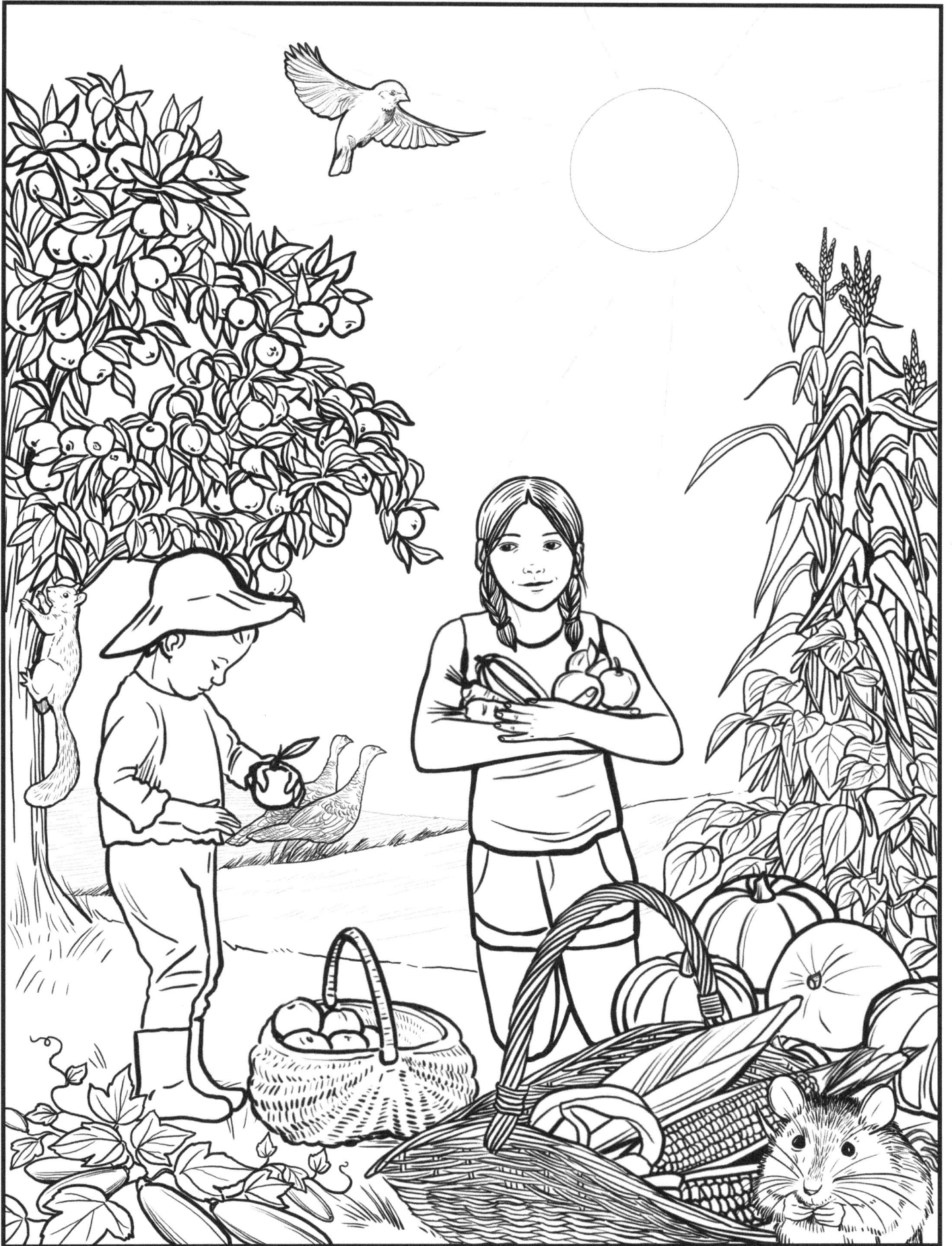

Before the winter snows arrive, the world is alight in color. Cottonwoods and aspens display their yellows, oranges, and golds. Many birds like blue herons, wood ducks, and trumpeter swans are headed south, while beavers prepare their home for winter.

Have you found fall mushrooms?
Or seen the beautiful red berries of uva-ursi?

Common English Names	Latin Binomial	nsəlxcin
Black cottonwood	*Populus balsamifera*	mulx
Trembling aspen	*Populus tremuloides*	məlməltiłp
Uva-ursi	*Arctostaphylos uva-ursi*	
Great blue heron	*Ardea herodias*	sk̓ʷas
Osprey	*Pandion haliaetus*	
Wood duck	*Aix sponsa*	x̌ʷʕatx̌ʷət
Trumpeter swan	*Cygnus buccinator*	spəqmix
Beaver	*Castor canadensis*	stunx

Not everyone sleeps through the night.

Who roams at night near you?
Do you hear the wolf howl?
The owl hoot?

A full moon lights up the sky, shedding light on those silently prowling.
Soon, dawn will arrive and it will be time for them to rest.

Sleep well, bobcat. Sleep well, fisher.

Common English Names	Latin Binomial	nsəlxcin
Ocean spray	*Holodiscus discolor*	
Snowberry	*Symphoricarpos albus*	təmtəmniłp
Snowbrush	*Ceanothus velutinus*	
Northern pygmy-owl	*Glaucidium gnoma*	snína?
Common raven	*Corvus corax*	yutəlxʷ
Pine siskin	*Carduelis pinus*	
Grey wolf	*Canis lupus*	nċi?cən
Fisher	*Martes pennanti*	ċix̌ʷċəx̌ʷ
Bobcat	*Lynx rufus*	ṗkam

About the Authors

Rosalee de la Forêt

Rosalee has spent over two decades wandering the meeting place between the wild and the tended, where plants and people come alive together. A lifelong lover of the green world, she's known for her grounded humor, practical insights, and boundless curiosity about the way herbs weave their healing into our lives. She finds daily inspiration in the beauty of the Methow Valley, where she has lived for nearly twenty years, marveling at the way plants make the ordinary extraordinary. Through her online school, books, and podcast, she invites others to join her in a hands-on exploration of herbalism that blends tradition, science, and a dash of wonder. HerbsWithRosalee.com

Xavier de la Forêt

Disillusioned with the state of Western civilization, Xavier spent years exploring different ways of living and found hope and solace in the wisdom of indigenous people. After learning an array of ancestral skills, he has been living in the Methow Valley for close to twenty years and has been focused on being a good caretaker for the land he calls home.

Caitlin Cordell

One of the most influential books in Caitlin's childhood was *Miss Rumphius*, a children's picture book about a woman who sought a way to make the world more beautiful and found it in planting lupines in the wild. The simple phrase "making the world more beautiful" has been an essential ethos for how Caitlin moves in work and life. After twenty years of youth and young adult centered community social work, Caitlin transitioned to being a full-time tattoo artist and illustrator. Her work is a practice in reverence towards the flora and fauna kin we live alongside. Combining her background in social work with her love of flora and fauna illustration is one way Caitlin hopes her art and connection with clients and community makes the world a little more beautiful. This naturalist coloring book was such an amazing learning experience that brought her closer to seeing the incredible ecosystem she is privileged to live within.

Acknowledgements

The seed ideas for this coloring storybook were planted during the memorial for beloved photographer Mary Kiesau. Mary was a naturalist, plant lover, photographer, and friend who was deeply rooted in the Methow Valley community. Those first ideas were vague, but we knew from the start that it would involve a community of people to make this book a reality.

As the ideas continued to germinate, it became clear that Caitlin Cordell would be a wonderful artist to bring our vision to fruition. In the early days we would meet often with Caitlin in order to share our initial concepts for each page, inspired by our cherished landscapes, animals, and plants, throughout the seasons. Caitlin both enhanced and simplified our ideas to create artwork that captures the beauty we find here.

We were honored to work with Elaine Timentwa Emerson, a Methow descendent, traditional basketmaker, and language holder, so that we could include the original names of many of the beings represented in this book. Thank you to David LaFever for helping us make this connection.

Thank you to Joanna Bastian and Sandi Scheinberg for help with editing the text.

Thank you to the Mary Kiesau Community Fellowship fund for contributing to this project. And to Greg Wright for helping us turn this project into reality!

We knew from the beginning that this would be a non-profit venture. Our vision is that any revenue from retail sales will enable us to bring complimentary copies into our local elementary schools each year. We have initial schools in mind and hope to expand the offerings as sales permit. Additional revenue may also go to help fund children's outdoor programs.

◆

Whether you have bought this book or were gifted it, we thank you for being a part of this project! Our biggest hope is that this coloring storybook will simply be the beginning, inspiring people to explore and connect more deeply with the beautiful place we are blessed to call home.

www.ingramcontent.com/pod-product-compliance
Lightning Source LLC
Chambersburg PA
CBHW041431270326
41934CB00022B/3499